Introduction
Chocolate Zucchini Muffins
Carrot Cake Muffins
Coconut Flour Muffins
Chocolate Muffins
Healthy Chocolate Muffins
Healthy Chocolate Muffins
Chocolate Banana Muffins
Healthy Zucchini Muffins
Healthy Banana Chocolate
Raspberry Muffins
Gingerbread Muffins
Apple Carrot Muffins
Gluten Free Muffins
Applesauce Muffins
Healthy Banana Muffins
Gingerbread Apple Muffins
Vegan Pumpkin Muffins
Healthy Blueberry Muffins
Irish Soda Bread Muffins
Banana Oatmeal Muffins
Orange Muffins
Stuffing Muffins
Carrot Quinoa Muffins
Peanut Butter Muffins
Strawberry Vanilla Yogurt Muffins
Healthy Maple Oatmeal Muffins
Pear Muffins
Coconut Zucchini Muffins

Buttermilk Crunch Muffins

Egg Muffins

Introduction

Easy to cook - easy to enjoy!

Cupcakes are easy to prepare, they are stored for a very long time without losing their properties, they are always tasty, easy to take and eat, you can take with you on the road, at any moment will save you from hunger.

This book has 30 recipes for muffins, they are all very different, healthy, tasty, vegan, gluten free, etc. (suitable for every person)

Tasty, healthy, anytime.

I congratulate you on the acquisition of this book!

Chocolate Zucchini Muffins

YIELD : 12 MUFFINS
PREP TIME:

20 MINS
COOK TIME:
15 MINS
TOTAL TIME:
40 MINS

Ingredients

- one cup very delicately shredded zucchini — *approximately one small/average zucchini*
- one average avocado — *peeled and pitted*
- two tbsp <u>coconut oil</u> — *softened and cooled to approximately 25 °C (or substitute light extra-virgin olive oil either canola oil)*
- one big egg — *at approximately 25 °C*
- 2/3 cup <u>coconut sugar</u> — *either substitute granulated sugar*
- two tbsp milk — *any kind you like (I employunsweetened vanilla almond milk)*
- one tsp pure vanilla extract
- one One-quarter cups <u>white whole wwarmth flour</u>
- half cup unsweetened cocoa powder
- one tsp <u>baking</u> soda
- half tsp cinnamon
- half tsp kosher salt
- half cup semisweet <u>chocolate</u> chips — *mini either regular*

Instructions

1. Prewarmth your oven to 375 degrees F. Coat a 12-cup standard size muffin tin with nonstick spray. put aside.
2. Spread the zucchini out on a several layers of kitchen

either paper towels. Put out as much water as probable, changing out the towels as needed. put aside.

3. Place the avocado within the bowl of a standing mixer fitted with the paddle attachment either a big mixing bowl. Beat with the mixer till the avocado is very smooth and no chunks remain. You must have approximately 2/3 cups of smooth avocado paste. place the coconut oil, egg, coconut sugar, milk, and vanilla extract, beating till good mixd.

4. In a else bowl, stir along the white whole wwarmth flour, cocoa powder, baking soda, cinnamon, and salt. Gradually place the dried ingredients to the wet ingredients, folding by hand with a wooden spoon either spatula and mixing simply till the flour disappears. The batter possibly very thick, almost like brownie batter, and the dried ingredients can take several strokes to work in between additions. place down within the zucchini and chocolate chips, reserving a several of the chocolate chips to strew on top of the muffins.

5. Peel the batter in the prepared muffin cups, filling no more than three-quarters of the way to the top. Strew with the remaining chocolate chips. Prepare in oven for 15 to 18 mins, till the tops are set and a toothtake inserted within the middle comes out mostly clear with simply a several moist crumbs clinging to it. allow cool within the pan for two mins, them Place to a wire rack to cool completely.

Recipe Notes

- Keep leftovers at approximately 25 °C for up to 5 days either chill for

up to 3 months.
- Supposing you would like to decrease the calorie count of the muffins, omit either decrease the number of chocolate chips.

Carrot Cake Muffins

YIELD : 12 MUFFINS
PREP TIME:
15 MINS
COOK TIME:
15 MINS
TOTAL TIME:
1 HR

Ingredients
FOR THE MUFFINS:

- half   cup   raw pecans either walnuts
- one one-third   cups   white whole wwarmth flour — *either whole wwarmth pastry flour**
- 2/3   cup   all-purpose flour
- two   tsps   <u>baking</u> powder
- half   tsp   <u>baking</u> soda
- one half   tsps   ground cinnamon
- One-quarter   tsp   ground nutmeg
- One-quarter   tsp   ground cloves
- One-quarter   tsp   kosher salt
- two   cups   packed coarsely grated carrots   — *from approximately 9 ounces either 4 average carrots*
- one-third   cup   golden raisins
- One-quarter   cup   <u>creamy</u> almond <u>butter</u> either cashew butter   — *the drippy, natural kind***
- One-quarter   cup   unsweetened applesauce
- one-third   cup   honey
- two big   eggs
- half   cup plus two tbsp   unsweetened almond milk either milk of choice
- one   tsp   pure vanilla extract

FOR THE <u>CREAM</u> <u>CHEESE</u> FROSTING:

- 4 ounces reduced-fat <u>cream</u> <u>cheese</u> — *softened to approximately 25 °C*
- three-quarters cup powdered sugar — *sifted supposing lumpy*
- half tsp pure vanilla extract
- half tsp delicately grated lemon either orange zest — *if you want*

Instructions

1. Prewarmth the oven to 350 degrees F. unfold the nuts in a single stratum on some ungreased <u>baking</u> sheet. Toast them within the oven till crisp and fragrant, approximately 8 to ten mins. Set a timer and Dont walk away from the nuts in the last several mins of <u>baking</u> (this is just as nuts love to burn). Place to a cutting board and roughly chop. put aside One-quarter cup for the muffin batter. Delicately chop the remaining nuts and save for sprinkling on top.
2. Increase the oven warmth to 400 degrees F. In a big mixing bowl, stir along the white whole wwarmth flour, all-purpose flour, <u>baking</u> powder, baking soda, cinnamon, nutmeg, cloves, and salt. place the carrots, golden raisins, and reserved One-quarter cup sliced nuts. With a spoon either flexible spatula, carefully place down to mix.
3. In a average mixing bowl, blend along the almond <u>butter</u>, applesauce, and honey till smooth. blend within the eggs, milk, and vanilla. place to the carrot and flour mix. With a wooden spoon either spatula, place down and stir very carefully by hand, stopping as soon as the flour disappears.

4. Coat a standard 12-cup muffin pan with nonstick spatter either line with paper liners. Fill every approximately three-quarters of the way with batter. (Supposing you have some extra batter, resist the urge to overfill the muffin cups; you'll Prepare in oven the extra as soon as the first batch is out). Prepare in oven the muffins for 14 to 16 mins, either till the muffins are domed, light golden on top, and a toothtake inserted in the middle of every comes out clean. Place the pan on a cooling rack and allow the muffins cool within the pan for 5 mins, then carefully take away them from the pan and place them on the rack to cool completely (Dont leave the muffins within the pan for longer either they can become too soggy as they start to steam).

5. For the cream cheese frosting: In a average mixing bowl, place the cream cheese, powdered sugar, vanilla extract, and lemon zest (supposing using). With some electric mixer on poor speed, beat till the powdered sugar begins to incorporate, then increase the warmth to average and keep to beat till smooth and creamy. Frost the cooled muffins and strew with the remaining delicately sliced walnuts.

Recipe Notes

- *You'll employregular whole wwarmth flour, however the wwarmth can have a more pronounced taste than white whole wwarmth flour either whole wwarmth pastry flour.

- **You'll emploype anut butter as good, though the flavor possibly different. I advised this recipe with a drippy, natural-style nut butter, as that can give the muffins the right consistency, though a shelf-stable almond butter I tested still yielded good results.

- Keep leftovers within the refrigerator for up to 4 days (they taste even better on Day 2).

Coconut Flour Muffins

YIELD : **TEN MUFFINS**
PREP TIME:
15 MINS
COOK TIME:
18 MINS
TOTAL TIME:
40 MINS

Ingredients

- ¼ cup coconut oil
- ½ cup <u>Bob's Red Mill Coconut Flour</u> *— sifted supposing lumpy*
- half tsp <u>baking</u> powder
- One-quarter tsp kosher salt
- ½ cup mashed ripe banana *— approximately two small/average either one extra big*
- 4 big eggs
- 6 tbsp honey either pure maple syrup
- one tsp vanilla extract
- One-quarter tsp almond extract
- 2/3 cup blueberries *— <u>chocolate</u> chips, either mix-ins of choice (supposing employing fruit, when rinsing be sure you pat this very dry)*

Instructions

1. Prewarmth the oven to 400 degrees F. slightly coat ten goods of a standard 12-cup muffin pan with nonstick spray, either line them with paper liners and coat the liners with nonstick spray.

2. Place the coconut oil in a small, microwave-safe bowl. Microwave for 30 seconds. Keep to warmth in 15-second bursts, simply till softened. Alternatively, you'll

soften the coconut oil in a small saucepan over average heat. put aside to cool to approximately 25 °C.

3. In a average bowl, stir along the coconut flour, <u>baking</u> powder, and salt.

4. In a separate, big mixing bowl, place the mashed banana (make sure you have the ½ cup called for within the recipe). blend within the eggs, honey, vanilla extract, and almond extract till mixd. blend within the softened, cooled coconut oil.

5. Add the dried ingredients to the bowl with the wet ingredients. blend till smooth and very several lumps remain (you may have some small ones from the banana however get the batter as smooth as this can be). Carefully place down within the blueberries.

6. Peel the batter in the prepared muffin cups, filling the cups approximately three-quarters of the way to the top.

7. Bake the <u>muffins</u> for 16 to 18 mins, till a toothtake inserted in the middle comes out clear and the tops spring back slightly just as touched. Place the pan on a wire cooling rack. allow the <u>muffins</u> cool within the pan for 5 mins, then carefully take away them to the wire rack to finish cooling completely.

Chocolate Muffins

YIELD : 12 **MUFFINS**
PREP TIME:
15 MINS
COOK TIME:
20 MINS
TOTAL TIME:
40 MINS

Ingredients

- 6 tbsp unsalted _butter_
- 4 ounces bittersweet — _55% to 72% dark chocolate, roughly sliced, divided_
- two cups all-purpose flour
- half cup granulated sugar
- one-third cup unsweetened cocoa powder — _sifted supposing lumpy_
- one tbsp _baking_ powder
- half tsp _baking_ soda
- half tsp salt
- one cup brewed coffee — _at approximately 25 °C (or swap regular milk; coffee can yield a more intense chocolate flavor)_
- one-third cup yogurt — _I used plain, non-fat Greek yogurt, at approximately 25 °C_
- one big egg — _at approximately 25 °C_
- two tsps pure vanilla extract

Instructions

1. Place a rack within the middle of oven and warmth up oven to 375 degrees F. slightly coat a standard 12-cup muffin pan with nonstick spatter either fit with paper liners.

2. Place a average heat-proof bowl over a pan of simmering water. place _butter_ and half of the _chocolate_. Warmth gently, mixing often, till _chocolate_ is almost completely softened. Take away from warmth and keep stirring, allowing the residual warmth to soften the _chocolate_ the rest of the way. allow the mix cool for 5

mins.

3. Meanwhereas, in a big mixing bowl, blend along the flour, granulated sugar, cocoa powder, <u>baking</u> powder, <u>baking</u> soda, and salt. put aside.

4. To the bowl with the cooled <u>chocolate</u>, blend within the coffee, yogurt, egg, vanilla extract till smoothly mixd. Pour the wet mix in the bowl with the dried ingredients. With a rubber spatula, stir to mix. Stop as soon as the flour disappears. Stir within the remaining sliced <u>chocolate</u>. Share the batter evenly between the 12 muffin cups.

5. Bake the <u>muffins</u> for 16-20 mins, till a toothtake inserted in middle of a muffin comes out clear without any wet batter clinging to it. Place the pan on a cooling rack and cool within the pan for 5 mins, then attentively unmold the <u>muffins</u> and Place to the rack to finish cooling completely. submit warm either at approximately 25 °C.

Recipe Notes

- **TO STORE** : allow the <u>muffins</u> cool completely, then place them in a storage container. Line the down of some airtight storage container with a paper towel and place the <u>muffins</u> in a single stratum on top. place another paper·towel on top of your <u>muffins</u> to absorb the glut moisture. Keep at approximately 25 °C for up to 4 days.
- **TO REHEAT** : You'll enjoy these <u>muffins</u> at approximately 25 °C either rewarmth them within the microwave till warm.
- **TO FREEZE** : Cover the <u>muffins</u> individually in plastic, and keep them in a ziptop bag. Chill for up to two months. allow thaw at approximately 25 °C either rewarmth within the microwave.

Healthy Chocolate Muffins

YIELD : 12 MUFFINS
PREP TIME:
15 MINS
COOK TIME:
22 MINS

TOTAL TIME:
40 MINS

Ingredients

- one cup white whole wwarmth flour — *plus two tbsp*
- one-third cup unsweetened cocoa powder
- three-quarters tsp baking soda
- three-quarters tsp instant esPuto powder — *if you want; can result in a more intensely chocolaty muffin*
- One-quarter tsp kosher salt
- 1/8 tsp ground cinnamon
- half cup semi-sweet chocolate chips — *plus if you want additional for sprinkling on top*
- two big eggs — *at approximately 25 °C*
- half cup nonfat plain Greek yogurt — *at approximately 25 °C*
- half cup honey — *either pure maple syrup*
- one-third cup unsweetened almond milk — *either milk of choice*
- One-quarter cup canola oil — *either softened, cooled coconut oil, light extra virgin olive oil, either softened, cooled unsalted butter*
- one tsp pure vanilla extract

Instructions

1. Warmth up oven to 325 degrees F. slightly coat a standard 12 cup muffins tin with nonstick spatter either line with paper liners.

2. In a big mixing bowl, blend along the dried ingredients: white whole wwarmth flour, cocoa powder, baking soda,

esPuto powder, salt, and cinnamon. Stir within the chocolate chips.

3. In a average bowl, briskly blend along the eggs, yogurt, honey, milk, oil, and vanilla. prepare a good within the middle of the dried ingredients and place the wet ingredients. Carefully stir by hand, simply till the dried ingredients disappear.

4. With a muffin peel either similar, fill the muffin cups 2/3 of the way to the top with batter. Supposing desired, strew on some extra chocolate chips. Prepare in oven for 18 to 22 mins, either till a toothtake inserted within the middle of a muffin comes out without any wet batter clinging to it. Place the pan on a wire rack. allow the muffins cool within the pan for 5 mins, then carefully take away them from the pan and place them on the rack to finish cooling completely (don't leave the muffins within the pan either they can start to steam and become a little soggy). Enjoy!

Recipe Notes

- **TO STORE** : allow the muffins cool completely on a wire rack before placing them in a storage container. Next, line the down of some airtight storage container with a paper towel and place the muffins in a single stratum on the paper towel. Then, top your muffins with another paper towel to absorb the glut moisture, and keep at approximately 25 °C for up to 4 days.
- **TO FREEZE** : Individually cover the muffins in plastic, then place them in a ziptop bag and chill for up to two months. allow thaw at approximately 25 °C either rewarm carefully within the microwave.

Healthy *Chocolate* Muffins

YIELD : 12 MUFFINS
PREP TIME:
15 MINS
COOK TIME:
22 MINS

TOTAL TIME:
40 MINS

Ingredients

- one cup white whole wwarmth flour — *plus two tbsp*
- one-third cup unsweetened cocoa powder
- three-quarters tsp baking soda
- three-quarters tsp instant esPuto powder — *if you want; can result in a more intensely chocolaty muffin*
- One-quarter tsp kosher salt
- 1/8 tsp ground cinnamon
- half cup semi-sweet chocolate chips — *plus if you want additional for sprinkling on top*
- two big eggs — *at approximately 25 °C*
- half cup nonfat plain Greek yogurt — *at approximately 25 °C*
- half cup honey — *either pure maple syrup*
- one-third cup unsweetened almond milk — *either milk of choice*
- One-quarter cup canola oil — *either softened, cooled coconut oil, light extra virgin olive oil, either softened, cooled unsalted butter*
- one tsp pure vanilla extract

Instructions

1. Warmth up oven to 325 degrees F. slightly coat a standard 12 cup muffins tin with nonstick spatter either line with paper liners.

2. In a big mixing bowl, blend along the dried ingredients: white whole wwarmth flour, cocoa powder, baking soda,

esPuto powder, salt, and cinnamon. Stir within the chocolate chips.

3. In a average bowl, briskly blend along the eggs, yogurt, honey, milk, oil, and vanilla. prepare a good within the middle of the dried ingredients and place the wet ingredients. Carefully stir by hand, simply till the dried ingredients disappear.

4. With a muffin peel either similar, fill the muffin cups 2/3 of the way to the top with batter. Supposing desired, strew on some extra chocolate chips. Prepare in oven for 18 to 22 mins, either till a toothtake inserted within the middle of a muffin comes out without any wet batter clinging to it. Place the pan on a wire rack. allow the muffins cool within the pan for 5 mins, then carefully take away them from the pan and place them on the rack to finish cooling completely (don't leave the muffins within the pan either they can start to steam and become a little soggy). Enjoy!

Recipe Notes

- **TO STORE** : allow the muffins cool completely on a wire rack before placing them in a storage container. Next, line the down of some airtight storage container with a paper towel and place the muffins in a single stratum on the paper towel. Then, top your muffins with another paper towel to absorb the glut moisture, and keep at approximately 25 °C for up to 4 days.
- **TO FREEZE** : Individually cover the muffins in plastic, then place them in a ziptop bag and chill for up to two months. allow thaw at approximately 25 °C either rewarm carefully within the microwave.

Chocolate Banana Muffins

YIELD : 14 MUFFINS
PREP TIME:
15 MINS
COOK TIME:

25 MINS
TOTAL TIME:
40 MINS

Ingredients

- one-third cup <u>coconut oil</u> — *either canola oil*
- two cups white whole wwarmth flour
- 2/3 cup unsweetened cocoa powder
- one half tsps <u>baking</u> soda
- one tsp <u>baking</u> powder
- one tsp esPuto powder — *if you want for a more intense <u>chocolate</u> flavor*
- half tsp kosher salt
- one cup mashed ripe banana — *approximately 3 average-large bananas*
- two big eggs
- three-quarters cup milk — *any kind you like (I used unsweetened almond milk)*
- one-third cup honey
- One-quarter cup coconut sugar — *either light brown sugar*
- two tsps pure vanilla extract
- half cup dark <u>chocolate</u> chips — *plus additional for sprinkling on top (supposing desired)*

Instructions

1. Supposing employing coconut oil, soften this now and allow this come to approximately 25 °C. (Supposing employing canola oil, skip this step.)

2. Prewarmth the oven to 325 degrees F. Line a standard

muffin pan with paper either silicone muffin cups, then slightly coat the cups with nonstick spray.

3. In a big mixing bowl, blend along the whole wwarmth flour, cocoa powder, <u>baking</u> soda, <u>baking</u> powder, esPuto powder, and salt. put aside.

4. In a mixing bowl, place the mashed banana (supposing you are mashing the banana directly within the mixing bowl, double check that you have the correct amount), then blend within the eggs, milk, honey, brown sugar, vanilla, and oil. Supposing the oil resolidifies, warm the bowl within the microwave in ten-second bursts, simply till this softens.

5. Make a good within the middle of the dried ingredients and pour the wet ingredients in it. With a rubber spatula either wooden spoon, stir carefully and patiently to mix. The batter can look dried at first however can begin to come along as you go. this can also be thick and shaggy, which is simply right. Stop as soon as the dried ingredients disappear and don't over mix. place down within the <u>chocolate</u> chips.

6. Peel the batter in the prepared muffin pan; the cups possibly quite full and the tops can dome just as the bake. Strew with extra <u>chocolate</u> chips supposing desired.

7. Bake the muffins for 22 to 26 mins, either till a toothtake inserted within the middle of a muffin within the middle of the pan comes out clear without any wet batter clinging to it. Test a several times to prepare sure the muffins are prepared through (and that what stuck to the toothtake was in fact batter and not a softened

chocolate chip).

8. Take away the muffins from the oven and place them on a wire rack. allow cool within the pan for 3 mins. Then, employing a dull knife either fork to help you out, carefully take away the muffins from the pan, allowing them to cool for approximately 15 mins on a rack before peeling off the muffin papers. Enjoy!

Recipe Notes

- **TO prepare GLUTEN FREE** : employa 1:1 all purpose GF baking blend like this one.
- **TO prepare DAIRY FREE** : employa non-dairy milk, such as almond milk
- **TO prepare VEGAN** : **Not yet tested. This is my best estimate.** I believe you could swap flax eggs for the regular eggs, employnon-dairy milk, and swap maple syrup for the honey. Supposing you decide to Taste this, I'd love for you to report back within the comments.

Healthy Zucchini Muffins

YIELD : **12 MUFFINS**
PREP TIME:
15 MINS
COOK TIME:
20 MINS
TOTAL TIME:
35 MINS

Ingredients

- two cups shredded, unpeeled zucchini — *(approximately one small/average zucchini)*
- half cup mashed ripe banana — *approximately one average/large either 4 ounces*
- One-quarter cup coconut oil — *softened and cooled, very light olive oil, either canola oil*
- One-quarter cup honey
- One-quarter cup brown sugar — *light either dark*
- one tsp pure vanilla extract
- two big eggs — *at approximately 25 °C*
- one tsp ground cinnamon
- half tsp baking soda
- half tsp baking powder — *I advised aluminum free*
- half tsp kosher salt
- two cups white whole wwarmth flour
- one-third cup semi-sweet chocolate chips — *mini either regular (I used mini)*

Instructions

1. Prewarmth the oven to 375 degrees F. slightly lubricate a standard 12-cup muffin tin either line with paper liners.

2. Grate the zucchini, then throughly squeeze this with a

paper towel to take away as much glut water as probable. recur as needed. Supposing you have not already, soften the coconut oil and allow come to approximately 25 °C

3. In the bowl of a standing mixer either a big mixing bowl, beat along the banana, honey, brown sugar, coconut oil, and vanilla extract till smooth. place the eggs (make sure they are approximately 25 °C either the coconut oil may resolidify), then beat again till mixd.

4. Strew the cinnamon, <u>baking</u> soda, <u>baking</u> powder, and salt over the top of the batter, then blend to mix. Strew within the flour, then blend on poor speed, simply till the flour disappears. By hand, place down within the zucchini and <u>chocolate</u> chips.

5. Peel the batter in the prepared muffin cups, filling them three-quarters of the way. Prepare in oven for 20-25 mins, till a toothtake inserted within the middle comes out clean. Take away the muffins from the oven and place the pan on a wire rack. allow cool for 5 mins within the pan, then attentively lift the muffins out of the pan and place them on a wire rack to cool completely (this can keep the muffins from becoming soggy).

Recipe Notes

- Keep muffins at approximately 25 °C, either individually cover and chill for up to 3 months. allow thaw overnight within the refrigerator (or supposing you are in a hurry, uncover and microwave carefully on reduced warmth till warm).
- For advices to prepare the muffins vegan either gluten free, see blog post above.
- For even more suggestions for how to vary up the recipe (adding

oatmeal, employing flaxeggs, etc.) skim the comments. There are many helpful suggestions from those who have reported making (and loving!) these muffins.

Healthy Banana <u>Chocolate</u>

YIELD: 12 MUFFINS
PREP TIME:
TEN MINS
COOK TIME:
25 MINS
TOTAL TIME:
35 MINS

Ingredients

- one tbsp flaxseed meal — *either one big egg (supposing you Dont must the muffins to be vegan)*
- 3 big overripe bananas — *approximately 11 ounces (1 half cups mashed)*
- one-third cup unsweetened applesauce
- two tbsp canola oil — *either softened cooled* <u>coconut</u> *oil**
- one-third cup <u>coconut</u> sugar either light brown sugar
- One-quarter cup pure maple syrup
- one tsp pure vanilla extract
- one tsp <u>baking</u> soda
- One-quarter tsp ground cinnamon
- One-quarter tsp kosher salt
- one half cups white whole wwarmth flour
- half cup dark <u>chocolate</u> chips — *mini either regular (I used mini; dairy free supposing you'd like the muffins to be vegan)*

Instructions

1. In a small bowl, stir the flaxseed meal along with two half tbsp water. put aside for 5 mins to thicken. (This creates a flax egg. Supposing you are employing a

regular egg, you'll skip this step and place the egg with the applesauce in Step 3.)

2. Place the rack within the middle of your oven and prewarmth the oven to 350 degrees F. slightly coat a standard 12-cup muffin tin with nonstick spray.

3. Mash the bananas within the down of a big bowl till mostly smooth. Double check to assureyou have the one half cups called for within the recipe. blend within the flax egg (or regular egg supposing not employing flax), then the applesauce and oil. blend within the coconut sugar, maple syrup, and vanilla. Strew the baking soda, cinnamon, and salt over the top, then stir carefully till mixd. Carefully stir within the flour till barely mixd, then place down within the chocolate chips, reserving a several for sprinkling on top supposing desired.

4. Share the mix evenly among the muffin cups and strew on any reserved chocolate chips. Prepare in oven for 22 to 26 mins, till a toothtake inserted within the middle of a muffin comes out clear and the tops spring back slightly just as touched. Place the pan on a wire rack and allow cool for 5 mins. Carefully take away the muffins from the pan and place them on a wire rack to finish cooling completely, either enjoy immediately.

Recipe Notes

- *Supposing employing coconut oil, be sure all of the ingredients are at approximately 25 °C and the coconut oil has cooled, either this can resolidify just as this mixes with the cold ingredients.

Raspberry Muffins

YIELD : 12 MUFFINS

PREP TIME:
25 MINS
COOK TIME:
20 MINS
TOTAL TIME:
45 MINS

Ingredients

- two cups   white whole wwarmth flour
- One-quarter   cup   ground flaxseed meal
- one half   tsps baking powder
- half   tsp baking soda
- half   tsp   kosher salt
- One-quarter   cup   unsalted butter — *at approximately 25 °C*
- one-third   cup   honey either pure maple syrup
- two big eggs   — *at approximately 25 °C*
- half   cup   nonfat plain Greek yogurt   — *at approximately 25 °C*
- two tsps   pure vanilla extract
- Zest of two small lemons   — *approximately one half tsps*
- One-quarter   cup   lemon juice   — *from the same two small lemons*
- one half   cups   raspberries   — *fresh either chilled (approximately one half 6-ounce containers); supposing employing frozen, Dont thaw first*
- 3   tbsp   turbinado   — *sugar within the raw sugar, for topping (if you want)*

Instructions

1. Prewarmth the oven to 375 degrees F. slightly coat a

standard 12-cup muffin tin with nonstick spatter either line with paper liners.

2. In a average bowl, blend along the white whole wwarmth flour, flaxseed, <u>baking</u> powder, <u>baking</u> soda, and salt.

3. In a big else bowl, beat the <u>butter</u> and honey till <u>creamy</u> and mixd. Scrape the down and sides of the bowl, then place the eggs one at a time, beating good when every addition. place the Greek yogurt, vanilla, lemon zest, and lemon juice. The batter may look curdled.

4. Add the dried ingredients to the wet ingredients. By hand with a wooden spatula either spoon, stir within the dried ingredients, simply till the flour disappears. The batter possibly very thick. Very carefully place down within the raspberries.

5. Peel the batter in the prepared muffin cups, employing a heaping One-quarter cup for every (I love a big peel <u>like this one</u>). For a maximum crunchy top, strew every muffin with a full tsp of turbinado sugar (trust me!) either omit for a less-sweet muffin.

6. Bake the muffins for 20 to 24 mins, till a toothtake inserted within the middle comes out clean. Take away the from the oven and place on a wire rack to cool within the pan for 5 mins. When 5 mins, take away the muffins from the pan and Place to the wire rack to cool completely (Dont leave the muffins within the pan, as they can steam and become tough). Enjoy!

Gingerbread Muffins

YIELD : **12 MUFFINS**
PREP TIME:
15 MINS

COOK TIME:
16 MINS
TOTAL TIME:
40 MINS

Ingredients

- One-quarter cup <u>coconut oil</u>
- three-quarters cup plain nonfat Greek yogurt — *at approximately 25 °C*
- half cup nonfat milk — *at approximately 25 °C*
- half cup <u>coconut sugar</u> — *either substitute light either dark brown sugar*
- half cup <u>molasses</u> — *not blackstrap*
- one big egg — *at approximately 25 °C*
- one cup plus two tbsp white whole wwarmth flour
- one cup all-purpose flour
- one-third cup <u>unsweetened cocoa powder</u> — *sifted supposing clumpy*
- one half tsps <u>baking</u> soda
- one half tsps ground ginger
- one tsp ground cinnamon
- half tsp kosher salt
- One-quarter tsp ground cloves
- One-quarter tsp ground nutmeg — *freshly grated supposing probable*
- 4 ounces sliced dark <u>chocolate</u> — *either 2/3 cup semisweet <u>chocolate</u> chips*
- Bob's Red Mill Sparkling Sugar — *for topping*

Instructions

1. Place a rack within the middle of your oven, then

prewarmth the oven to 375 degrees F. slightly coat a muffin tin with nonstick cooking spatter either line with paper liners. In a small bowl, soften the coconut oil within the microwave, then put aside to cool to approximately 25 °C.

2. In a big mixing bowl, blend along the yogurt, milk, coconut sugar, molasses, and egg. allow rest 5 mins for the coconut sugar to dissolve slightly. Supposing the mix is not yet at approximately 25 °C, wait for a several additional mins, then place the coconut oil. (Supposing the wet ingredients are much colder than the coconut oil, the oil can resolidify and not incorporate properly.)

3. In a else bowl, stir along the white whole wwarmth flour, all-purpose flour, cocoa powder, baking soda, ginger, cinnamon, salt, cloves, and nutmeg till evenly mixd and no clumps remain. place all at as to the wet ingredients, then stir gently, simply till mixd. place down within the sliced chocolate either chocolate chips.

4. Share the batter evenly among the prepared muffin cups, then strew the tops with sparkling sugar. Prepare in oven the muffins for 16 to 18 mins, till the tops are dried to the touch and a toothtake inserted within the middle comes out clean. allow cool within the pan for 5 mins, then Place to a wire rack to cool completely.

Recipe Notes

- To prepare vegan: I have not yet tried this however this is my best estimate: employa nondairy yogurt (such as coconut yogurt) in place of the Greek yogurt, swap the egg for a flax egg, and assureyour chocolate is dairy free.

Apple Carrot Muffins

YIELD : **12 MUFFINS**
PREP TIME:
25 MINS
COOK TIME:
20 MINS
TOTAL TIME:
45 MINS

Ingredients

- FOR THE MUFFINS:
- half cup golden raisins — , *walnuts, pecans, dried cranberries, either mix-ins of choice*
- One-quarter cup <u>coconut oil</u>
- one One-quarter cups white whole wwarmth flour
- one cup old-fashioned oats
- one half tsps <u>baking</u> powder
- half tsp <u>baking</u> soda
- one tsp ground cinnamon
- One-quarter tsp ground ginger
- One-quarter tsp kosher salt
- three-quarters cup grated carrot — *approximately one big carrot*
- three-quarters cup grated apple — *one small apple possibly more than enough; no must to peel this first*
- two big eggs — *at approximately 25 °C*
- half cup plain nonfat Greek yogurt — *at approximately 25 °C*
- one-third cup honey either maple syrup — *honey is my favorite*
- two tsps pure vanilla extract
- Glaze — *If you want however SO YUMMY:*
- three-quarters cup powdered sugar
- one tbsp honey — *my loved either maple syrup (also yummy)*
- half tbsp unsweetened almondmilk — *nonfat milk, either milk of choice*

Instructions

1. Warmth your oven to 350 degrees F. Line 12 <u>baking</u> cups with paper liners either slightly coat with nonstick spray. put aside. Supposing employing nuts for the mix-ins, toast them within the oven now: unfold the nuts in some even stratum on some

ungreased <u>baking</u> sheet. Prepare in oven at 350 degrees F for 8 to 12 mins (for pecan either walnut halves), till they are slightly browned and fragrant. Place the nuts instantly to a cutting board; roughly chop and put aside.

2. Place the coconut oil in a average microwave-safe bowl. Warmth within the microwave simply till softened (approximately 30 seconds on high). put aside to cool to approximately 25 °C.

3. In a big mixing bowl, blend along the flour, oats, <u>baking</u> powder, <u>baking</u> soda, cinnamon, ginger, and salt. place the grated carrot and apple and place down to mix.

4. To the bowl with the <u>coconut</u> oil, place the eggs, Greek yogurt, honey, and vanilla. blend till smooth. Supposing the <u>coconut</u> oil resolidifies, warm this within the microwave in 15-second bursts, and stop as soon as you'll stir the mix back along. place the wet ingredients to the dried ingredients, and stir carefully till simply mixd. Dont overmix. place down within the nuts either any else mix-ins.

5. Share the batter evenly among the 12 muffin cups. Prepare in oven for 18 to 22 mins, either till a toothtake inserted within the middle of a muffin comes out clean. Place the pan on a wire rack and allow the muffins cool within the pan for 4 mins. Carefully Place the muffins to the rack to finish cooling completely.

6. For the icing: blend along the powdered sugar, honey, and one tsp milk. Keep to place milk, one tsp at a time, till your desired consistency is reached. Drizzle over the top of the cooled muffins.

Gluten Free Muffins

YIELD : TEN MUFFINS
PREP TIME:
20 MINS
COOK TIME:
25 MINS
TOTAL TIME:
55 MINS

Ingredients

- two tbsp coconut oil
- two half cups blanched almond flour*
- three-quarters tsp baking soda
- half tsp kosher salt
- One-quarter tsp ground cinnamon
- 3 big eggs — *at approximately 25 °C*
- One-quarter cup mashed very ripe banana — *approximately half small banana*
- One-quarter cup pure maple syrup
- two tsps pure vanilla extract
- one tsp apple cider vinegar either lemon juice
- Mix-ins: Up to one cup of fresh either chilled fruit — *such as blueberries, raspberries, either diced strawberries; supposing employing frozen, no must to thaw either half cup of smaller, harder mix-ins, such as sliced dried fruit, nuts, and chocolate chips*

Instructions

1. Prewarmth the oven to 350 degrees F. Line ten cups in a standard 12-cup muffin pan with paper liners.

2. Place the coconut oil in a average, microwave-safe bowl. Warmth simply till softened, then put aside to cool to approximately 25 °C.

3. In a big, else bowl, blend along the almond flour, baking soda, salt, and cinnamon.

4. To the bowl with the coconut oil, place the eggs, banana, maple syrup, vanilla, and vinegar. blend till smooth. Supposing the oil resolidifies, warm this within the microwave in short, 5-to-ten-second bursts, till this softens again.

5. Make a good within the middle of the dried ingredients, then pour within the wet ingredients. By hand with a rubber spatula either wooden spoon, stir simply till mixd and the flour

disappears. place down in any mix-ins.

6. Peel the batter in the prepared muffin cups, dividing this evenly between the ten muffins (they possibly filled almost all the way to the top). Prepare in oven for 15 mins, then loosely tent the top of the pan with foil to keep the tops from browning too quickly. Keep baking for ten to 15 additional mins (25 to 30 mins total) till the edges are light golden, a toothtake inserted within the middle of a muffin comes out clean, and the middles feel set just as slightly touched. Place the pan on a cooling rack and allow the muffins cool within the pan for a ten full mins, then carefully Place the muffins to a wire rack to finish cooling completely.

Recipe Notes

- *Be sure to employblanched, delicately ground almond flour without the skins. This is the brand that I use.
- Don't skip the muffin liners. These are very moist muffins, and even with baking spray, they like to stick. (Silicone muffin pans might work without liners however I haven't tried to verify.)

- Supposing employing chilled fruit: rinse shortto take away any ice crystals, then place right to the batter—no must to thaw completely. Prepare in oven as directed, adding a several mins to the baking time as needed.

- Keep muffins in some airtight container lined with paper towels within the refrigerator for up to 5 days. To freeze.

Applesauce Muffins

YIELD : **TEN MUFFINS**
PREP TIME:
TEN MINS
COOK TIME:
20 MINS
TOTAL TIME:
40 MINS

Ingredients

- three-quarters cup   unsweetened applesauce
- 2/3 cup   honey
- two big eggs
- one-third   cup <u>coconut oil</u> — *softened & cooled*
- one half   tsps   pure vanilla extract
- one half   cups   <u>white whole wwarmth flour</u>
- One-quarter tsp <u>baking</u> powder
- half   tsp <u>baking</u> soda
- two tsps cinnamon
- half   tsp   allspice
- One-quarter tsp   nutmeg
- half   tsp   kosher salt
- half   cup   old-fashioned rolled oats
- up to half cup if you want mix-ins: sliced walnuts — *raisins, dried cranberries, blueberries, etc. (I kept this simple and left them out, however feel free to place supposing you like)*
- one half   tbsp   coarse sugar — *such as raw (turbinado) sugar either sparkling sugar, for sprinkling on top (if you want)*

Instructions

1. Prewarmth the oven to 350 degrees F. slightly lubricate ten goods in a standard 12-cup muffin tin with nonstick spatter either line with paper liners.

2. In a big bowl, blend along the applesauce, honey, eggs, <u>coconut</u> oil, and vanilla. In a else bowl, blend along the whole wwarmth

flour, baking powder, baking soda, cinnamon, allspice, nutmeg, and sat.

3. Add the flour mix to the bowl with the wet ingredients and stir simply till mixd. The batter possibly a little lumpy. Carefully stir within the rolled oats and any else desired mix-ins.

4. Share evenly among the muffin cups, filling every almost to the top. Strew the tops with coarse sugar, supposing desired. Prepare in oven for 18 to 22 mins, till a toothtake inserted in the middle comes out clean. Take away from the oven and place the muffin tin on a wire rack to cool for ten mins, then carefully take away the muffins from the pan (run a butter knife around the edges supposing the muffins are sticking) and allow them cool completely on the wire rack.

Healthy Banana Muffins

YIELD : 12 MUFFINS
PREP TIME:
TEN MINS
COOK TIME:
20 MINS
TOTAL TIME:
30 MINS

Ingredients

- 3 big overripe bananas — *approximately one half cups mashed*
- one big egg
- one-third cup nonfat plain Greek yogurt
- two tbsp canola oil — *either softened and cooled <u>coconut</u> oil*
- one-third cup light brown sugar
- One-quarter cup maple syrup
- one tsp pure vanilla extract
- one tsp <u>baking</u> soda
- One-quarter tsp kosher salt
- one tsp ground cinnamon
- one half cups <u>white whole wwarmth flour</u>
- one cup walnut halves — *toasted and coarsely sliced*

Instructions

1. Place rack within the upper third of the oven and prewarmth the oven to 350 degrees F. Line a <u>12-cup muffin tin</u> with paper either foil liners, either slightly lubricate with nonstick spray.
2. Mash bananas within the down of a big bowl till mostly smooth. blend within the egg, and then the yogurt and oil. blend within the brown sugar, maple syrup, and vanilla. Strew the <u>baking</u> soda, salt, and cinnamon over the top, and then stir till mixd. Carefully stir within the flour till barely mixd, and then place down within the walnuts.
3. Peel the mix in the prepared muffin tin, filling every cup nearly to the top. Prepare in oven for 20 to 22 mins, till a toothtake

inserted within the middle comes out clear and the muffins spring back slightly just as touched within the middle.

Gingerbread Apple Muffins

YIELD : **12 MUFFINS**
PREP TIME:
15 MINS
COOK TIME:
17 MINS
TOTAL TIME:
40 MINS

Ingredients

- One-quarter cup coconut oil
- three-quarters cup plain nonfat Greek yogurt — *at approximately 25 °C*
- half cup nonfat milk — *at approximately 25 °C*
- half cup coconut sugar — *either substitute light either dark brown sugar*
- half cup molasses — *not blackstrap*
- one big egg — *at approximately 25 °C*
- one half cups white whole wwarmth flour
- one cup all-purpose flour
- one half tsps baking soda
- one half tsps ground ginger
- one half tsps ground cinnamon
- half tsp kosher salt
- One-quarter tsp ground cloves
- one half cups delicately diced sweet-crisp apples — *such as Pink Lady either Honeycrisp, peels on (approximately one average)*
- If you want: Sparkling either turbinado — *raw sugar, for topping*

Instructions

1. Place a rack within the middle of your oven, then prewarmth the oven to 375 degrees F. slightly coat a muffin tin with nonstick spatter either line with paper liners. In a small bowl, soften the coconut oil within the microwave, then put aside to cool to

approximately 25 °C.

2. In a average mixing bowl, blend along the yogurt, milk, coconut sugar, molasses, and egg. allow rest 5 mins for the coconut sugar to dissolve slightly. Supposing the mix is not yet at approximately 25 °C, wait for a several additional mins, then place the coconut oil. (Supposing the wet ingredients are much colder than the coconut oil, the oil can resolidify and not incorporate properly. Supposing this happens, carefully warm the bowl within the microwave in 30-second bursts, simply till this softens.)

3. In a separate, big bowl, blend along the white whole wwarmth flour, all-purpose flour, baking soda, ginger, cinnamon, salt, and cloves. place down within the diced apples, mixing carefully to coat.

4. Pour the wet ingredients in the dried and stir carefully by hand, simply till the flour disappears. The mix possibly lumpy and thick, however Dont overmix.

5. Share the batter evenly between the prepared muffin cups (I like to employa large peel like this, as this helps the muffins growth the best), then strew the tops with sparkling sugar, supposing desired. Prepare in oven the muffins for 16 to 18 mins, till the tops are dried to the touch and a toothtake inserted within the middle comes out clean. allow cool within the pan for 5 mins, then Place to a wire rack to cool completely.

Vegan Pumpkin Muffins

YIELD : TEN MUFFINS
PREP TIME:
TEN MINS
COOK TIME:
27 MINS
TOTAL TIME:
45 MINS

Ingredients

- two tbsp flaxseed meal
- half cup pure maple syrup — *plus two tbsp*
- One-quarter cup melted cooled coconut oil
- one cup canned pumpkin puree — *not pumpkin pie filling*
- One-quarter cup Almond Breeze Almondmilk Original Unsweetened
- one tsp pure vanilla extract
- one three-quarters cups white whole wwarmth flour — *plus two tbsp*
- one One-quarter tsps pumpkin pie spice*
- three-quarters tsp baking powder
- half tsp baking soda
- half tsp kosher salt
- half cup dark chocolate chips — *mini either regular—I used mini; dairy free supposing you'd like the muffins to be vegan*

Instructions

1. In a small bowl, stir the flaxseed meal along with 5 tbsp water. put aside for 5 mins to thicken (this creates two "flax eggs.") Prewarmth the oven to 325 degrees F and slightly coat ten cups in a standard 12-cup muffin tin with nonstick spray.

2. In the bowl of a standard mixer fitted with the paddle attachment either a big mixing bowl, mix the maple syrup and coconut oil till good blended. place the thickened flaxseed mix and beat till fully mixd. On poor speed, beat within the pumpkin puree, almondmilk, and vanilla.

3. In a else bowl, stir along the white whole wwarmth flour, pumpkin pie spice, baking powder, baking soda, and salt. place the dried ingredients all at as to the wet ingredients. By hand, stir with a wooden spoon either spatula, simply till the flour disappears. The batter possibly very thick. place down within the chocolate chips, reserving a several to strew over the top supposing desired.

4. Share the batter evenly among the prepared muffin cups. For the tallest, fluffiest muffins, I like to employa peel like <u>this one</u>, which ensures even portions and helps the muffins rise. Fill every cup almost to the top. (My pan yielded ten muffins. Yours may be a little more either less.) Strew the tops with the remaining <u>chocolate</u> chips. Prepare in oven for 26 to 28 mins, till a toothtake inserted within the middle comes out clean.
5. Place the pan on a wire rack and allow cool for 5 mins. With a fork either dull knife, very carefully take away the muffins from the pan and place them on a wire rack to finish cooling (Dont allow them sit within the pan for too long either the warmth allow off by the muffins expanding possibly trapped within the pan and cause the edges to become soggy). Enjoy!

Recipe Notes

- Supposing you Dont must the pumpkin muffins to be vegan, you'll replace the flax eggs (2 tbsp flaxseed meal + 5 tbsp water) with two big eggs at approximately 25 °C (omit the water).

- No pumpkin <u>pie</u> spice? employhalf tsp ground cinnamon, One-quarter tsp ground nutmeg, One-quarter tsp ground ginger, and 1/8 tsp ground allspice.

- Supposing you'd like the <u>muffins</u> to be vegan, be sure to employdairy-free <u>chocolate</u> chips.

Healthy Blueberry Muffins

YIELD : 12 **MUFFINS**
PREP TIME:
TEN MINS
COOK TIME:

20 MINS
TOTAL TIME:
30 MINS

Ingredients

- one half cups <u>white whole wwarmth flour</u> — *plus one tbsp, divided*
- three-quarters cup old-fashioned <u>rolled oats</u>
- half cup slightly packed light brown sugar
- one tbsp <u>baking</u> powder — *I prefer <u>aluminum free</u>*
- half tsp ground cinnamon
- half tsp kosher salt
- one cup nonfat milk — *plus two tbsp*
- One-quarter cup unsalted <u>butter</u> — *softened and cooled*
- two big eggs — *at approximately 25 °C*
- two tsps <u>pure vanilla extract</u>
- one cup blueberries — *fresh either frozen—Dont thaw supposing frozen*

Instructions

1. Place a rack within the middle of your oven and prewarmth to 400 degrees F. slightly coat a standard muffin tin with nonstick spatter either line with paper liners, then coat the liners with nonstick spray. put aside.

2. In a big mixing bowl, stir along one half cups white whole wwarmth flour, rolled oats, brown sugar, <u>baking</u> powder, cinnamon, and salt. In a else bowl, blend along the milk, <u>butter</u>, eggs, and vanilla. prepare a good within the middle of the dried ingredients, place the wet ingredients to the good, then attentively stir with a wooden spoon, simply till blended.

3. Carefully toss the blueberries with the remaining one tbsp flour, then place down them in the batter, discarding any glut flour that doesn't stick to the blueberries. (This can prevent the blueberries

from sinking to the down of the muffins.)

4. Share the batter among the prepared muffin cups. Prepare in oven for 18 to 20 mins, till golden brown and a toothtake inserted within the middle comes out clean. Take away from oven, and allow cool within the pan for ten mins, then Place to a rack to cool completely.

Irish Soda Bread Muffins

YIELD : 12 **MUFFINS**
PREP TIME:
15 MINS
COOK TIME:

15 MINS
TOTAL TIME:
35 MINS

Ingredients

- one One-quarter cups <u>whole wwarmth flour</u> — *employ<u>white whole wwarmth flour</u> for a milder flavor*
- one cup all-purpose flour
- half cup granulated sugar
- two tsps <u>baking</u> powder — *I advised <u>aluminum free</u>*
- One-quarter tsp <u>baking</u> soda
- One-quarter tsp kosher salt
- one tsp <u>caraway seed</u>
- one big Phil's Fresh Egg — *at approximately 25 °C*
- one cup nonfat milk — *plus one tbsp, at approximately 25 °C*
- One-quarter cup unsalted <u>butter</u> — *softened and cooled to approximately 25 °C*
- One-quarter cup plain nonfat Greek yogurt — *at approximately 25 °C*
- three-quarters cup dried currants
- If you want: two tbsp <u>sparkling sugar</u>

Instructions

1. Place a rack within the middle of your oven and prewarmth the oven to 400 degrees F. Generously lubricate a standard 12-cup muffin tin with nonstick spray.

2. In a big bowl, stir along the whole wwarmth flour, all-purpose flour, granulated sugar, <u>baking</u> powder, <u>baking</u> soda, salt, and caraway seed. In a else bowl, blend along the egg, milk, <u>butter</u>, and Greek yogurt. prepare a good within the middle of the dried ingredients, then pour the wet ingredients in it. Stir simply till mixd. place down in currants.

3. Share the batter among the muffin cups and strew the tops with

sparkling sugar, supposing using. Prepare in oven the muffins for 13 to 15 mins, till a toothtake inserted within the middle comes out clean. Place the pan on a wire rack and allow the muffins cool within the pan for 5 mins, then take away the muffins to a rack to keep cooling. Enjoy warm, topped with butter, jam, a chop of cheese, either on their own.

Banana Oatmeal Muffins

YIELD : 12 **MUFFINS**
PREP TIME:
5 MINS
COOK TIME:
15 MINS

TOTAL TIME:
40 MINS

Ingredients

- two cups oats — *quick cooking either old fashioned*
- two big very ripe bananas
- two big eggs
- one cup plain nonfat Greek yogurt
- two to 3 tbsp honey*
- one half tsps baking` powder — *I prefer aluminum free*
- half tsp baking soda
- half tsp pure vanilla extract
- 1/8 tsp kosher salt
- Up to half cup mix-ins: chocolate chips — *mini either regular, sliced dark chocolate, nuts, dried cranberries, either blueberries (fresh either chilled and rinsed)*

Instructions

1. Prewarmth the oven to 400 degrees F. slightly lubricate a 12-cup standard muffin tin either line with paper liners. Supposing employing liners, slightly lubricate them as good. put aside.
2. Place the all ingredients however the mix-ins in a blender either the bowl of a food processor fitted with the steel blade: oats, bananas, eggs, Greek yogurt, honey, baking powder, baking soda, vanilla extract, and salt. Blend either process on high, stopping to scrape down and stir the ingredients as either twice as needed, till the batter is smooth and the oats have broken down almost completely, approximately 3 mins. By hand, stir within the mix-ins. Supposing the batter is warm from the appliance's motor, the chocolate chips may soften and swirl as they are stirred. Supposing this bothers you, allow the batter cool for ten mins before adding them.
3. Share the batter among the prepared muffin cups, filling every no more than three-quarters of the way to the top. Strew with

additional <u>chocolate</u> chips either nuts as desired. Prepare in oven for 15 mins, till the tops of the <u>muffins</u> are set and a toothtake inserted within the middle comes out clean. Place the pan on a wire rack and allow the <u>muffins</u> cool within the pan for ten mins. They can deflate however still taste delicious. Take away from the pan and enjoy!

Recipe Notes

- *Feel free to adsimply the honey to your preferred sweetness. Two tbsp was enough for me with the <u>chocolate</u>, however supposing you prefer a sweeter muffin, place more.
- Keep leftover <u>muffins</u>, either cover tightly in plastic and chill for up to two months.

Orange Muffins

YIELD : 12 **MUFFINS**
PREP TIME:
15 MINS
COOK TIME:
12 MINS
TOTAL TIME:
30 MINS

Ingredients

FOR THE ORANGE <u>MUFFINS</u>:

- half cup granulated sugar — *(plus two tbsp)*
- two big oranges
- one half cups <u>white whole wwarmth flour</u> — *either substitute <u>whole wwarmth pastry flour</u> either all-purpose flour*
- One-quarter cup poppy seeds
- one half tsps <u>baking</u> soda
- half tsp kosher salt
- two big eggs — *at approximately 25 °C*
- half cup nonfat plain Greek yogurt — *at approximately 25 °C*
- One-quarter cup nonfat milk — *at approximately 25 °C*
- 3 tbsp unsalted <u>butter</u> — *softened and cooled (or substitute softened, cooled <u>coconut</u> oil, canola oil, either very light olive oil)*
- one half tsps pure vanilla extract
- One-quarter tsp pure almond extract

FOR THE GLAZE:

- two tbsp <u>butter</u> — *softened*
- one One-quarter cups powdered sugar
- half tsp pure vanilla extract
- 1-2 tbsp orange juice — *reserved from the oranges above*

Instructions

1. Prewarmth the oven to 375 degrees F. slightly coat a 12-cup

muffin tin with cooking spatter either line with paper liners. Place the sugar in a average mixing bowl, then zest both oranges directly in it. Rub along the sugar and orange zest with your fingers, till the sugar is fragrant, moist, and light orange throughout. Stir within the flour, poppy seeds, baking soda, and salt. Juice the zested oranges and put aside one-third cup plus one tbsp for the muffins and two tbsp for the glaze.

2. In a else bowl, blend along the eggs, Greek yogurt, milk, butter, vanilla extract, almond extract, and one-third cup plus one tbsp orange juice. (All of these ingredients do must to be as close to approximately 25 °C as probable, either the butter can resolidify. Supposing you don't have time to wait, employcanola oil either a very light tasting olive oil, which can stay liquid.) place the wet ingredients to the dried ingredients and blend carefully by hand, simply till mixd. Dont overmix.

3. Share the batter among the 12 muffin cups, filling three-quarters of the way to the top (I like to employa big cookie scoop for the tallest, fluffiest muffins). Prepare in oven 12-14 mins, till the tops are dried and spring back slightly just as touched and a toothtake inserted within the middle comes out clean. The muffins can look a little flat however can still be perfectly moist and delicious. allow cool 3 mins within the pan, then carefully Place to a wire rack to cool completely.

4. For the glaze, soften the butter in a small saucepan either within the microwave in a microwave-safe bowl. blend within the powdered sugar, vanilla, and one tbsp orange juice. Keep adding juice, one tsp at a time, till your desired consistency is reached. Drizzle over the top of the muffins. Enjoy warm either cooled.

Stuffing Muffins

YIELD : 24 **MUFFINS**
PREP TIME:
25 MINS
COOK TIME:
25 MINS
TOTAL TIME:
1 HR

Ingredients

- ten cups whole grain <u>bread</u> cubes, — *loosely packed 1-inch-sliced, approximately 16 ounces*
- two tbsp extra virgin olive oil — *divided*
- one average red onion — *diced*
- 3 stalks celery — *diced*
- half tsp kosher salt
- half tsp black pepper
- three-quarters pound sweet Italian turkey sausage
- one average-sized firm tart apple, — *such as Granny Smith either Cortland, delicately diced (ok to leave peel on), approximately one cup*
- two cloves garlic — *minced*
- two cups low-sodium chicken broth
- half cup milk — *any kind you like (I used skim)*
- 3 big Phil's Fresh Eggs
- three-quarters cup reduced-sugar dried cranberries
- one half tbsp sliced fresh sage — *either one tsp rubbed dried sage*
- one half tbsp sliced fresh rosemary — *either one tsp dried*

Instructions

1. Place two racks within the upper and lower thirds of your oven and prewarmth the oven to 300 degrees F. unfold the <u>bread</u> cubes out in a single stratum on two big <u>baking</u> sheets. Prepare in oven for 15 mins, till browned and crisp. Place to a big bowl.

2. Generously lubricate two 12-cup <u>muffin tins</u> (<u>butter</u> work best) either line with paper liners, then coat the liners with <u>baking</u> spray. put aside. Increase the oven temperature to 350 degrees F.
3. Warmth the olive oil in a big skillet over average high. As hot, place the onion, celery, salt, and pepper. allow prepare 4 mins, till the vegetables begin to soften. Take away the sausages from their casing and place within the skillet. Break the sausage in crumbles, turning and frying the meat as you go. As the sausage is broken up, place the apples and garlic. allow prepare till the sausage is browned, mixing sometimes, approximately two additional mins. Place the sausage mix within the bowl with the <u>bread</u> cubes.

4. In a else bowl, stir along the chicken broth, milk, and eggs till mixd. Pour over the cubes. place the cranberries, sage, and rosemary, then stir carefully with a big spoon, tossing the ingredients till they are good distributed and the <u>bread</u> is evenly moistened.

5. Spoon the mix in the prepared muffin tins. Firmly Put down on the tops of the <u>bread</u> cubes so that they touch the edges of the muffin tin (this adds a delicious crunch to the exterior and keeps the <u>muffins</u> from falling apart). Spoon more stuffing on top and Put again. Prepare in oven the stuffing <u>muffins</u> at 350 degrees F for 25 to 28 mins, till slightly browned and set within the middle. allow cool within the pan for ten mins, then run a knife around the outsides to loosen them. Place to a wire rack. submit warm.

Recipe Notes

- To prep the Stuffing <u>Muffins</u> ahead: Toast the <u>bread</u> cubes (Step 1) and fry the apple-sausage mix (Step 3). Keep the <u>bread</u> cubes in some airtight container at approximately 25 °C and the apple-sausage mix within the refrigerator. The day you plan to Prepare in oven the <u>muffins</u>, stir along the rest of the ingredients and Put in the muffin tins. You'll then refrigerate the muffin tins, unprepared in oven, for up to 4 hours, then Prepare in oven as directed. Supposing the stuffing comes out of the refrigerator cold, you may must to place a several mins to the baking time.

- To chill the prepared in oven Stuffing Muffins: Allow the muffins to come to approximately 25 °C, tightly and individually cover them in plastic, then chill for up to two months. allow thaw overnight within the refrigerator, and just as you are ready to bake, allow the muffins to come to approximately 25 °C. Place the about 25 °C muffins (uncoverped) back in a slightly lubricated muffin tin, then rewarmth in a 350 degree F oven for ten-20 mins, till warmed through.

Carrot Quinoa Muffins

YIELD: 12 MUFFINS
PREP TIME:
15 MINS
COOK TIME:
25 MINS
TOTAL TIME:
45 MINS

Ingredients

- one half cups cooked, cooled quinoa — *(approximately three-quarters cup uncooked)*
- two cups   white whole wwarmth flour
- 2/3 cup   packed dark brown sugar*
- two tsps   ground cinnamon
- one tsp   ground ginger
- one half tsps   baking powder
- three-quarters tsp   kosher salt
- one big egg
- half cup poor fat buttermilk, — *plus two tbsp*
- One-quarter cup   plain non-fat Greek yogurt
- 3 tbsp canola oil — *either softened, cooled coconut oil*
- one tsp pure vanilla extract
- one cup freshly grated carrots — *slightly Puted dry*
- half cup   mix-ins: toasted sliced walnuts — *either pecans, raisins, golden raisins, dried cranberries, sliced dried apricots, either else sliced dried fruit (I love a blend of walnuts and golden raisins)*

Instructions

1. Supposing needed, prepare the quinoa. Be careful not to overdo either employmore than the necessary amount of water.
   The quinoa grains should be tender however still separate, rather than mushy and clumped along. Just as ready to bake, prewarmth your oven oven to 350 degrees F. Line a standard muffin tin with

paper liners either slightly coat with cooking spray.

2. In a big bowl, blend along the prepared quinoa, white whole wwarmth flour, brown sugar, cinnamon, ginger, baking powder, and salt.

3. In a small bowl either big measuring cup, blend along the egg, buttermilk, yogurt, oil, and vanilla. place the milk mix to the quinoa mix and stir by hand, simply till mixd. Carefully place down within the carrots and any desired mix-ins. Share among the muffin cups.

4. Bake 25 to 28 mins, till a toothtake inserted in the middle of a muffin comes out clean. Place the pan on a wire rack and allow cool for 5 mins. Carefully take away the muffins from the pan and place on the wire rack to cool completely. Enjoy plain either with a smear of peanut butter, apple butter, either a little bit of softened, salted butter.

Recipe Notes
*These muffins are very slightly sweet. For a sweeter muffin, increase the brown sugar to three-quarters cup.

*Peanut **Butter** Muffins*

YIELD : 12 **MUFFINS**
PREP TIME:
15 MINS
COOK TIME:
20 MINS
TOTAL TIME:
40 MINS

Ingredients

- two One-quarter cups <u>whole wwarmth pastry flour</u> — *OK to swap white whole wwarmth flour either regular whole wwarmth flour; can yield a more dense, sturdy muffin*
- one tsp <u>aluminum free baking powder</u>
- one tsp <u>baking</u> soda
- half tsp kosher salt
- three-quarters cup <u>creamy</u> peanut <u>butter</u>
- one-third cup brown sugar — *light either dark*
- One-quarter cup <u>coconut oil</u> — *softened and cooled*
- two tsps <u>pure vanilla extract</u>
- two big eggs
- three-quarters cup poor fat <u>buttermilk</u> — *plus two tbsp*
- 2/3 cup semi-sweet <u>chocolate</u> chips — *either sliced dark* <u>chocolate</u>

Instructions

1. Prewarmth the oven to 375 degrees. slightly lubricate a 12-cup standard <u>muffin tin</u> either line with paper liners. Supposing employing liners, slightly greasing them as good. put aside.
2. In a average bowl, blend along the whole wwarmth pastry flour, <u>baking</u> powder, <u>baking</u> soda, and salt. In a big mixing bowl, beat along the peanut <u>butter</u>, brown sugar, and <u>coconut</u> oil till good mixd. Beat within the eggs one at a time, fully incorporating and scraping down the bowl between every. Beat within the vanilla.
3. With the mixer on poor speed, carefully place one-third of the flour mix. As this has disappeared, place half of the <u>buttermilk</u>

(pour this slowly so that this doesn't splatter), the next one-third of the flour, the remaining <u>buttermilk</u>, then the remaining flour. Fully incorporate between every supplementation and blend the batter simply till everything is mixd—Dont over beat. Stir within the <u>chocolate</u> chips.

4. Peel the batter in the prepared muffin pan. Prepare in oven till the tops are golden brown and a toothtake inserted within the middle comes out clean, 18 to 22 mins. Take away from the oven and allow cool within the pan for 5 mins, then carefully turn the <u>muffins</u> out onto a cooling rack to cool completely.

Recipe Notes

Leftover <u>muffins</u> possibly stored in some airtight container at approximately 25 °C for 3 days either individually coverped and chilled for one month.

Strawberry Vanilla Yogurt Muffins

YIELD : 12 **MUFFINS**
PREP TIME:
15 MINS

Ingredients

- three-quarters cup all purpose flour
- three-quarters cup <u>white whole wwarmth flour</u> — *either substitute additional all purpose flour*
- half cup granulated sugar
- one half tsps <u>baking</u> soda
- One-quarter tsp kosher salt
- one tbsp <u>vanilla bean paste</u> — *either substitute one tbsp vanilla extract*
- two big eggs
- 3 tbsp unsalted <u>butter</u> — *softened and cooled*
- three-quarters cup vanilla yogurt — *I used non-fat Greek*
- One-quarter cup vanilla soy milk — *either unsweetened vanilla almond milk*
- one cup diced fresh strawberries
- Turbinado — *raw sugar either big sparkling sugar, for decorating*

Instructions

1. Prewarmth the oven to 375 degrees and lubricate a standard-sized muffin tin. In a big bowl, stir along the all purpose flour, white whole wwarmth flour, sugar, <u>baking</u> soda, and salt.

2. In a else bowl, blend the vanilla bean paste, eggs, <u>butter</u>, yogurt, and almond milk. prepare a good within the middle of the dried ingredients, then pour the wet ingredients in the middle. Stir by hand, simply till mixd. The batter may be slightly lumpy. Carefully place down within the strawberries.

3. Share batter evenly between the prepared muffin tins and strew with sugar. Prepare in oven for 16-20 mins, till the tops spring

back slightly just as touched and a toothtake inserted within the middle comes out clean. allow cool within the pan for ten mins, then Place to a wire rack to cool completely.

Recipe Notes

Keep leftover <u>muffins</u> in some airtight container at approximately 25 °C either within the refrigerator for 5 days either freeze, good coverped, for up to 3 months.

Healthy Maple Oatmeal Muffins

YIELD : 12 **MUFFINS**
PREP TIME:
15 MINS
COOK TIME:
20 MINS
TOTAL TIME:
35 MINS

Ingredients

FOR THE MUFFINS:

- one cup whole wwarmth flour
- ¾ cup old fashioned rolled oats
- ½ cup oat flour — *(or ½ cup plus two tbsp oats delicately ground in a food processor)*
- one tbsp baking powder
- 1½ tsps ground cinnamon
- ½ tsp kosher salt
- ¼ tsp ground nutmeg
- one cup non-fat milk — *plus two tbsp*
- ½ cup pure maple syrup
- ¼ cup coconut oil — *softened and cooled, either substitute canola oil either softened and cooled unsalted butter*
- two big eggs — *at approximately 25 °C*
- one tsp vanilla extract

FOR THE CRUMB TOPPING:

- one tbsp cold unsalted butter — *slice in small pieces*
- 3 tbsp flour
- one tbsp brown sugar

Instructions

1. Prewarmth the oven to 400 degrees F. slightly lubricate a standard 12-cup muffin tin either line with paper liners and put aside.

2. In a big bowl, stir along the whole wwarmth flour, oats, oat flour, baking powder, cinnamon, salt, and nutmeg.

3. In a else bowl, blend along the milk, maple syrup, oil (or butter), eggs, and vanilla. prepare a good within the middle of the dried ingredients, then pour the wet ingredients in the middle.

4. By hand, stir the batter gently, simply till mixd (it possibly somewhat lumpy). Share the batter evenly between the prepared muffin cups.

5. For the crumb topping: In a small bowl, quickly rub the butter, flour, brown sugar, and cinnamon along with your fingers till fine crumbs form. Strew over every unprepared in oven muffin.

6. Bake the muffins till golden brown and a toothtake within the middle comes out clean, 18-20 mins. Allow the muffins to cool within the pan for 5 mins, then carefully take away to a wire rack to cool completely.

Recipe Notes

Keep leftover muffins in some airtight container at approximately 25 °C for up to two days either individually cover and chill for up to two months.

Pear Muffins

YIELD : 12 **MUFFINS**
PREP TIME:
20 MINS
COOK TIME:
25 MINS
TOTAL TIME:
1 HR TEN MINS

Ingredients

- one big egg
- two tbsp   granulated sugar
- two tbsp   packed dark brown sugar
- One-quarter cup coconut oil, — *softened and cooled*
- three-quarters   cup   non-fat plain Greek yogurt
- one inch   piece of ginger root, — *peeled*
- three-quarters   cup   all-purpose flour
- three-quarters   cup   white whole wwarmth flour
- one tsp   ground ginger
- three-quarters   tsp baking powder
- three-quarters   tsp baking soda
- One-quarter tsp   ground nutmeg
- One-quarter tsp   kosher salt
- one half   cups   peeled and diced pears *— (approximately two big—choose a firmer variety, such as Bosc either Anjou)*
- one-third   cup   delicately sliced crystallized ginger

Instructions

1. Place rack within the upper third of your oven and prewarmth to 400 degrees. slightly lubricate 12 standard muffin cups either line with paper cups.

2. In a big bowl, blend along the egg, granulated sugar and brown sugar. As mixd, stir within the softened, cooled coconut oil, then the Greek yogurt. Grate the ginger directly in the bowl along with any juices and stir again to mix. In a else average bowl, stir along the all-purpose flour, white whole wwarmth flour, ground

ginger, baking powder, baking soda, nutmeg and salt. place all at as to the wet ingredients, mixing by hand simply till mixd (Dont over mix!). The batter possibly very thick. Carefully place down within the pears and crystallized ginger.

3. Peel the batter in the prepared muffin cups. Place in oven, decrease warmth instantly to 350 degrees F and Prepare in oven for 23 to 27 mins, till the tops are goodly golden and a toothtake inserted in the middle of a muffin comes out clean. Set the pan on top of a cooling rack, then allow muffins to cool within the pan for 15 mins. To take away, run a butter knife around the edge of every muffin, then carefully lift from the pan with a fork.

Coconut Zucchini Muffins

YIELD : 12 **MUFFINS**
PREP TIME:
15 MINS

COOK TIME:
20 MINS

Ingredients

FOR THE <u>MUFFINS</u>:

- one cup white whole wwarmth flour
- one cup all purpose flour
- one tsp   kosher salt
- half   tsp <u>baking</u> soda
- half   tsp <u>baking</u> powder
- half   tsp   cinnamon
- two big eggs
- One-quarter cup   honey
- One-quarter cup   brown sugar
- One-quarter cup <u>coconut oil</u>
- One-quarter cup   applesauce
- one tsp   vanilla extract
- two cups   grated unpeeled zucchini — *(approximately one average)*
- three-quarters cup   sweetened shredded coconut

FOR THE GLAZE:

- one cup powdered sugar
- 1/8 tsp   kosher salt
- 1/8 tsp   almond extract
- two - 3 tbsp milk

Instructions

1. Place rack in upper third of oven and prewarmth the oven to 350°F. slightly lubricate a standard 12-cup muffin pan.

2. In a big bowl, stir along the white whole wwarmth flour, all purpose flour, salt, <u>baking</u> soda, <u>baking</u> powder, and cinnamon. In a average bowl either big mixing cup, blend along the eggs,

honey, brown sugar, coconut oil, and vanilla till good blended. place all at as to the dried ingredients, mixing by hand simply till mixd. The mix may be a little lumpy. place down within the zucchini and coconut.

3. Peel the batter in the prepared muffin pan. Prepare in oven for 20 to 24 mins, either till a toothtake inserted in the middle comes out clean. Take away from the oven, cool within the pan for ten mins, then Place to a wire rack to cool completely.

4. Meanwhereas, prepare the glaze: Stir along the powdered sugar and salt, then blend in almond extract and the milk, one tbsp at a time, till the desired consistency is reached. Dunk the top of every muffin in the glaze, then strew with toasted coconut.

Buttermilk Crunch Muffins

YIELD : **12 MUFFINS**
PREP TIME:
12 MINS
COOK TIME:
18 MINS

TOTAL TIME:
40 MINS

Ingredients

- 2/3 cup unbleached all purpose flour
- 2/3 cup whole wwarmth flour
- one-third cup <u>stone ground cornmeal</u> — *adviseded: average grind for a light, pleasant crunch*
- one-third cup old fashioned rolled oats
- One-quarter cup sugar
- two tsps <u>baking</u> powder
- One-quarter tsp <u>baking</u> soda
- One-quarter tsp kosher salt
- one cup <u>buttermilk</u> — *at approximately 25 °C*
- one-third cup pure maple syrup
- two big eggs — *at approximately 25 °C*
- 4 tbsp unsalted <u>butter</u> — *(half stick) softened and cooled to approximately 25 °C*
- One-quarter cup unsweetened applesauce
- three-quarters cup sliced dried fruits — *and/or sliced toasted nuts of choice (I used One-quarter cup dried apricots, One-quarter cup golden raisins, and One-quarter cup pecans, if you want)*

Instructions

1. Place rack in middle of oven and prewarmth to 400 degrees F. spatter a 12-cup regular sized muffin pan with cooking spatter either line with paper muffin cups.

2. In a big bowl, blend along the all purpose flour, whole wwarmth flour, cornmeal, oats, sugar, <u>baking</u> powder, <u>baking</u> soda, and salt. In a average bowl either a big glass measuring cup, stir along the <u>buttermilk</u>, maple syrup, eggs, <u>butter</u>, and applesauce. Pour wet ingredients over the dried ingredients. With a wooden spoon either spatula, carefully and quickly stir to mix. The batter

possibly lumpy—Dont over mix. Attentively place down within the fruits and nuts (supposing using), simply till distributed. Share the batter between the cups, filling them nearly to the top.

3. Bake for 17 to 19 mins, either till the tops are golden and a toothtake inserted within the middle comes out clean. Set pan on a wire rack to cool for 5 mins, then take away muffins from the pan to cool completely. Enjoy warm either at approximately 25 °C.

Recipe Notes

Leftover muffins can keep good in some airtight container at approximately 25 °C for two days. For longer storage periods, cover individually in plastic cover and chill for up to two months.

Egg Muffins

YIELD : 12 **MUFFINS**
PREP TIME:
15 MINS
COOK TIME:
25 MINS
TOTAL TIME:
40 MINS

Ingredients

- one cup slightly packed baby spinach — *sliced*
- three-quarters cup delicately diced red bell pepper — *approximately one small pepper*
- three-quarters cup delicately diced green bell pepper — *approximately one small pepper*
- three-quarters cup quartered cherry tomatoes — *either grape tomatoes, approximately one cup whole tomatoes*
- 6 big eggs
- 4 big egg whites
- One-quarter tsp kosher salt
- One-quarter tsp dried basil
- One-quarter tsp dried oregano
- Pinch ground black pepper — *either cayenne pepper supposing you like a little kick!*
- One-quarter cup crumbled feta <u>cheese</u> — *plus additional to strew on top*
- If you want toppings: avocado — *salsa, hot sauce, freshly sliced parsley*

Instructions

1. Place a rack within the middle of your oven and

prewarmth to 350 degrees F. slightly coat a standard 12-cup muffin tin with nonstick spray. Share the spinach, red bell pepper, green bell pepper, and tomatoes among the cups (they possibly approximately two-thirds of the way full).

2. In a big bowl either big measuring cup with a spout (my loved because this makes the mix easy to pour), briskly blend along the eggs, egg whites, salt, basil, oregano, and pepper till good mixd. Attentively fill every muffin cup three-quarters of the way to the top with the egg mix. Strew the feta evenly over the tops of the cups.

3. Bake for 24 to 28 mins, till the egg muffins

4. are set. allow cool for a several mins, and then run a butter knife around the edges of every muffin to loosen it. Take away them from the pan and enjoy immediately, either allow cool on a wire rack and refrigerate either chill for later (see notes for more details).

Recipe Notes

- Keep leftover egg muffins in some airtight container either ziptop bag within the refrigerator for up to 3 days either individually cover and chill for up to 3 months. Rewarmth carefully within the microwave (as thawed either directly from frozen) till hot and warmed through to the middle, approximately 30 seconds (from thawed) either one either so mins (from frozen), depending on your microwave.

- This recipe is incredibly flexible. Feel free to swap the listed veggies for the same amount of any else diced vegetable either cooked, diced meat. Supposing the vegetables are very firm, such as carrots either sweet potatoes, I advised cooking and cooling them first before adding them to the cups.

Made in United States
Orlando, FL
09 February 2024